Building A Unified, Happy Home: A Guide to Blended Families

Alan Ford

Published by Alan Ford, 2024.

BUILDING A UNIFIED, HAPPY HOME: A GUIDE TO BLENDED FAMILIES

First edition. August 17, 2024.

Copyright © 2024 Alan Ford.

ISBN: 979-8227823885

Written by Alan Ford.

Table of Contents

Preface

In 2002, as a divorced dad with primary custody of two sons (ages 2 and 4), I met a wonderful woman from another state who had primary custody of two daughters (ages 8 and 15). We married, combined our households, and welcomed a son in 2005. Today, only our youngest son lives at home while attending college; the other four have moved out, with three married, and we have five grandsons. Reflecting on our journey, I appreciate how most people never realized we were a blended family. This book aims to help blended families navigate complexities and achieve a loving, unified family.

INTRODUCTION TO
BLENDED FAMILIES
WELCOME
WELCOME
CHAPTER 1
BLENDED
FAMILIES

Chapter 1: Introduction

Overview of Blended Families

Blended families, sometimes referred to as stepfamilies, are becoming increasingly common in today's society. These families form when one or both partners in a couple bring children from previous relationships into their new partnership. Blended families can include various configurations, such as parents with children from prior marriages, single parents who marry, or even families where partners choose to cohabit without marrying but still blend their households.

In these families, members must navigate the complexities of new relationships while maintaining connections with former partners, extended family, and step-siblings. This dynamic can present unique challenges but also offers immense opportunities for growth, love, and the creation of a larger support network.

Importance of Creating a Unified, Happy Home

A unified and happy home is crucial for the well-being of all family members. Children in blended families often face significant adjustments, and a harmonious home can provide them with the stability and security they need to thrive. For adults, fostering a cohesive family unit can reduce stress and strengthen their relationship.

Creating unity in a blended family involves building trust, establishing clear communication, and fostering mutual respect. When family members feel valued and understood, they are more likely to cooperate and support each other. This supportive environment can enhance the emotional and psychological health of everyone involved, leading to a happier and more resilient family.

Goals and Structure of the Book

The primary goal of this book is to provide practical advice and strategies for families navigating the challenges of blending households. It aims to equip readers with the tools they need to create a loving, supportive, and unified family environment.

The book is structured to address the various stages and aspects of blending families, from the initial transition to ongoing relationship building and conflict resolution. Each chapter offers insights, tips, and real-life examples to help readers apply the concepts to their own lives.

Here's a breakdown of what you can expect in each chapter:

1. **Understanding Blended Families**: An in-depth look at the different types of blended families and the unique dynamics they bring.
2. **Preparing for the Transition**: Guidance on how to prepare yourself and your children for the changes that come with blending families.
3. **Strategies for Smooth Transitions**: Practical tips for easing the transition and helping family members adjust to the new family structure.
4. **Mastering Co-Parenting**: Strategies for effective co-parenting, including communication techniques and conflict resolution.
5. **Building Strong Relationships**: Activities and practices to help family members bond and build strong, healthy relationships.
6. **Addressing Common Challenges**: Solutions for common issues faced by blended families, such as jealousy, financial strain, and external influences.
7. **Celebrating Diversity and Unity**: Ways to embrace the diversity within your family and celebrate your unique family culture.
8. **Glossary of Key Terms**: Definitions of important terms and concepts related to blended families.
9. **Conclusion**: A recap of the key points and encouragement for the journey ahead.

At the end of each chapter, you will find recommended resources, such as books, articles, and websites, to further explore the topics discussed.

Recommended Material

To better understand the topics covered in this introduction, consider the following resources:

1. **Books:**
    a. **"The Smart Stepfamily: Seven Steps to a Healthy Family" by Ron L. Deal**
    b. **"Stepfamilies: Love, Marriage, and Parenting in the First Decade" by James H. Bray and John Kelly**
2. **Articles:**
    a. **"Blended Family and Step-Parenting Tips" by HelpGuide.org**
    b. **"10 Tips for a Healthy Blended Family" by PsychCentral**
3. **Websites:**
    a. **Stepfamily Foundation[1]**
    b. **National Stepfamily Resource Center[2]**

These materials provide additional insights and practical advice to help you navigate the complexities of blended families and create a happy, unified home.

---

1. https://www.stepfamily.org

2. http://www.stepfamilies.info

Chapter 2: Understanding Blended Families

Definition and Types of Blended Families

A blended family, also known as a stepfamily, forms when one or both partners in a relationship bring children from previous relationships into their new union. These families can take many shapes and sizes, reflecting the diversity and complexity of modern family life. Here are some common types of blended families:

1. **Traditional Blended Family**: This includes a married couple where one or both partners have children from previous marriages or relationships.
   a. **Dynamics:**
      i. **New Parental Roles**: In a traditional blended family, one or both partners bring children from previous marriages. This creates new roles, with one partner becoming a stepparent.
      ii. **Sibling Integration**: Children from different families must learn to coexist, share spaces, and build new sibling relationships.
      iii. **Shared Parenting Responsibilities**: Both parents share the responsibility of raising the children, which requires coordination and cooperation.
   b. **Challenges:**
      i. **Loyalty Conflicts**: Children might feel torn between their biological parent and stepparent, leading to loyalty conflicts.
      ii. **Discipline Differences**: Establishing consistent discipline can be challenging, especially if the biological and stepparents have different parenting styles.
      iii. **Bonding Time**: Creating opportunities for the new family members to bond and build relationships

        takes time and effort.

    iv. **Ex-Spouse Dynamics**: Managing relationships with ex-spouses can add stress, particularly if there are disagreements about parenting.

  c. **Example**: The Anderson family consists of a father with two children and a mother with one child. Initially, the children struggled with feelings of jealousy and competition. Through family meetings and setting clear rules, the Andersons gradually established a respectful and cooperative household.

2. **Cohabiting Blended Family**: Similar to the traditional blended family, but the partners are not married.

  a. **Dynamics:**

    i. **Non-Marital Partnership: In a cohabiting blended family, partners live together without being married. This dynamic can be more flexible but also less legally defined.**

    ii. **Informal Structures: The lack of formal marital commitment can lead to a more informal family structure, which can be both freeing and challenging.**

  b. **Challenges:**

    i. **Legal Ambiguities: Without the legal protections of marriage, partners may face challenges related to inheritance, healthcare decisions, and custody arrangements.**

    ii. **Social Acceptance: Depending on cultural and societal norms, cohabiting families may encounter judgment or lack of support.**

    iii. **Commitment Levels: Differences in perceived commitment can lead to insecurities or conflicts within the family.**

    iv. **Financial Arrangements: Managing finances and household responsibilities without the legal framework of marriage requires clear communication and agreements.**

    c. **Example:** The Harrisons decided to cohabit, bringing together the mother's daughter and the father's son. They faced criticism from extended family but focused on open communication and mutual support to strengthen their family bond.

3. **Single-Parent Blended Family**: One parent, with children from a previous relationship, marries or forms a partnership with another adult who may or may not have children.

    a. **Dynamics:**

        i. **Solo Parent Adjustment: A single parent brings a new partner into the family, requiring both the parent and the children to adjust to the new dynamic.**

        ii. **Enhanced Support: The new partner can provide additional support and resources, improving the family's overall well-being.**

    b. **Challenges:**

        i. **Trust Building: The single parent and children need time to trust the new partner and integrate them into the family.**

        ii. **Role Clarification: Clarifying the new partner's role in parenting and discipline can prevent conflicts and confusion.**

        iii. **Emotional Adjustment: The single parent and children may need time to emotionally adjust to the presence of a new adult in the home.**

        iv. **Co-Parenting with Biological Parent: Managing co-parenting responsibilities with the biological parent while integrating a new partner can be complex.**

    c. **Example:** Maria, a single mother of two, married John, who had no children. The children initially resisted John's involvement. Maria and John attended family therapy to develop strategies for building trust and establishing John's role in the family.

4. **Double-Blended Family**: Both partners bring children from previous relationships into the new family unit.

   a. **Dynamics**:

      i. **Complex Family Structure:** Both partners bring children from previous relationships, creating a larger, more complex family unit.

      ii. **Multiple Sibling Relationships:** Children must navigate relationships with multiple new siblings, each with their own personalities and needs.

   b. **Challenges**:

      i. **Integration of Many Members:** Integrating many family members requires patience and effort, as each person adjusts to the new dynamic.

      ii. **Fairness and Equity:** Ensuring all children feel equally valued and treated can be challenging, especially with different parenting histories.

      iii. **Space and Privacy:** Managing living space and ensuring everyone has enough privacy can be difficult in a larger household.

      iv. **Unified Family Identity:** Creating a unified family identity while respecting individual histories and relationships takes time.

   c. **Example:** The Johnsons merged two families with three children each. The children initially formed cliques based on their original families. Through family activities and counseling, they began to see themselves as a single unit, learning to appreciate and support one another.

Each type of blended family brings its own set of dynamics and challenges, but they all share the common goal of creating a loving, unified household.

Recommended Material

To gain deeper insights into the dynamics and challenges of different types of blended families, consider the following resources:

a. **Books:**
   i. "The Smart Stepfamily: Seven Steps to a Healthy Family" by Ron L. Deal
   ii. "Stepfamily Realities: How to Overcome Difficulties and Have a Happy Family" by Margaret Newman
b. **Articles:**
   i. "Blended Family and Step-Parenting Tips" by HelpGuide.org
   ii. "The Dynamics of Blended Families" by Psychology Today
c. **Websites:**
   i. Stepfamily Foundation[1]
   ii. National Stepfamily Resource Center[2]

These resources provide valuable guidance and practical advice to help you navigate the unique dynamics and challenges of blended families, ensuring a harmonious and happy home.

Statistics and Trends

Blended families are becoming more prevalent globally, reflecting significant shifts in societal norms, family structures, and marriage patterns. Understanding these trends is essential to recognizing the growing importance of addressing the unique needs of blended families.

Global Statistics and Trends

1. **Prevalence:** Blended families are increasingly common worldwide as divorce rates rise and people remarry or enter new partnerships. In many developed countries, the percentage of marriages that end in divorce is high, leading to a greater number of blended families.

---

1. https://www.stepfamily.org

2. http://www.stepfamilies.info

Globally, it is estimated that about 15-20% of children live in blended family arrangements, with significant regional variations.

2. **Marriage and Remarriage Rates**: The global divorce rate varies widely by region, but in many countries, second marriages are common following a divorce. However, the success rate of these remarriages is often lower than first marriages due to the additional challenges of blending families. For example, globally, it is estimated that around 50-60% of second marriages end in divorce.

3. **Children in Blended Families**: Across the world, children in blended families face unique challenges, such as adjusting to new parental figures, forming relationships with stepsiblings, and navigating complex family dynamics. These experiences are shaped by cultural norms, legal frameworks, and the availability of support systems for blended families.

United Kingdom Statistics and Trends

1. **Prevalence**: In the UK, blended families are also on the rise. Around 11% of couples with dependent children are stepfamilies, according to the Office for National Statistics (ONS). This trend is expected to grow as more people remarry or enter long-term cohabiting relationships after divorce or separation.

2. **Marriage and Remarriage Rates**: The UK has seen a steady increase in divorce rates over the past few decades, with approximately 42% of marriages ending in divorce. Remarriage is relatively common, with about 40% of all marriages in the UK involving at least one partner who has been married before. The success rate of these remarriages can be lower, often due to the added pressures of blending families.

3. **Children in Blended Families**: Around 8-10% of children in the UK live in blended families. These children often experience similar challenges to those in other countries, such as adjusting to new family structures and navigating relationships with stepparents and stepsiblings. However, the UK's social services and legal system offer various forms of support to help these families succeed.

United States Statistics and Trends

1. **Prevalence**: Blended families are one of the fastest-growing family types in the United States. Approximately 40% of families in the U.S. are blended, reflecting the high rate of divorce and remarriage in the country. This significant percentage highlights the need for tailored resources and support for these families.

2. **Marriage and Remarriage Rates**: In the U.S., about 50% of first marriages end in divorce, and around 60% of second marriages also end in divorce. The challenges of integrating children from previous relationships and managing complex family dynamics contribute to these statistics. Despite these challenges, many blended families successfully create stable and loving environments through effective communication and strong family bonds.

3. **Children in Blended Families**: Around 16% of children in the U.S. live in blended families. These children often encounter unique opportunities and challenges as they adapt to new family dynamics. The U.S. has a wide range of resources, including counseling and educational programs, to support children and parents in blended families.

Summary

These trends highlight the growing prevalence of blended families around the world and the importance of understanding their unique dynamics. While the challenges can be significant, many families successfully navigate these complexities, creating stable and loving homes. The statistics emphasize the need for continued support, research, and resources to help blended families thrive in today's ever-evolving social landscape.

The Dynamics of Blended Families

Blended families are unique in their dynamics, often characterized by a mix of excitement, challenges, and opportunities. Understanding these dynamics is crucial for creating a harmonious household, where all members feel valued and connected. Let's explore these dynamics in more detail.

Adjusting to New Roles

In a blended family, one of the first and most significant adjustments involves redefining roles and relationships. This process can be both exciting and challenging as each family member navigates their new place within the family structure.

1. **Parents as Stepparents**: Parents entering a new marriage or partnership must assume the role of a stepparent. This transition requires sensitivity and patience, as the stepparent must find a balance between offering guidance and support while respecting the established parent-child relationship. Stepparents often need to build their relationship with stepchildren gradually, earning trust and respect over time.

2. **Children Gaining Stepsiblings**: Children in blended families may find themselves with new siblings, which can be both a source of joy and tension. Adjusting to the presence of stepsiblings often involves navigating feelings of competition, jealousy, or even loss, especially if they are used to being the only child or the oldest sibling. It's important for parents to foster an environment where all children feel equally valued and supported.

3. **Adapting to Multiple Parental Figures**: In cases where both parents bring children into the relationship, children must adapt to having multiple parental figures. This can create confusion about authority and expectations, especially if parenting styles differ significantly between biological parents and stepparents. Consistent communication and setting clear expectations can help mitigate these challenges.

Building Trust

Trust is the foundation of any successful family, and in blended families, it plays an even more critical role. Building trust is a gradual process that requires time, effort, and consistency from all family members.

1. **Earning Trust**: For stepparents, earning the trust of stepchildren is

crucial. This involves being reliable, showing genuine interest in the child's life, and respecting the child's boundaries. Trust is not something that can be rushed; it must be developed naturally through positive and consistent interactions.

2. **Trust Among Siblings**: Trust among siblings, especially stepsiblings, is equally important. It is built through shared experiences, cooperation, and mutual respect. Encouraging siblings to work together on common goals, such as a family project or activity, can help foster this trust.

3. **Trust Between Parents**: Parents in a blended family must also build and maintain trust with each other, especially in matters of parenting and discipline. This trust is essential for presenting a united front and avoiding conflicts that could undermine the family's harmony.

Communication

Open and honest communication is the cornerstone of a harmonious blended family. It ensures that everyone's feelings, needs, and concerns are acknowledged and addressed, fostering an environment of understanding and cooperation.

1. **Expressing Feelings**: Family members should feel safe expressing their feelings, whether positive or negative. Encouraging children to share their thoughts about the changes in their family can prevent misunderstandings and help parents address any issues early on.

2. **Listening with Empathy**: Effective communication isn't just about speaking; it's equally about listening. Family members should practice active listening, showing empathy and understanding, especially when emotions run high. This approach helps validate each person's experiences and strengthens family bonds.

3. **Conflict Resolution**: In any family, conflicts are inevitable, but in a blended family, the stakes can be higher due to the complex dynamics. Clear and respectful communication is key to resolving conflicts. Setting aside time for family discussions or meetings can be a helpful strategy to address and resolve issues collectively.

Establishing Boundaries

Clear boundaries are essential in blended families to prevent misunderstandings and ensure that everyone feels respected and secure. These boundaries help define personal space, responsibilities, and acceptable behavior within the family.

1. **Respecting Personal Space**: In a blended family, where multiple people may be adjusting to living together, respecting each other's personal space is crucial. This might involve setting rules about privacy, such as knocking before entering a room, or allowing children to have time alone when needed.

2. **Defining Parental Roles**: It's important to clarify the roles of biological parents and stepparents. This includes understanding who will handle specific parenting responsibilities and how discipline will be managed. Clear boundaries in this area help avoid conflicts and ensure that children receive consistent guidance.

3. **Setting Behavioral Expectations**: Establishing clear rules and expectations for behavior within the household can help maintain harmony. This might include guidelines on chores, screen time, and respectful communication. Having these boundaries in place from the beginning helps create a stable and predictable environment.

Creating New Traditions

New family traditions are a powerful way to foster unity and create a sense of belonging in a blended family. These traditions provide opportunities for family members to bond and create shared memories.

1. **Simple Traditions**: Even small, simple traditions can have a big impact. For example, having a weekly family movie night, a Sunday brunch, or a special bedtime routine can create consistency and comfort for children and adults alike.

2. **Celebrating Milestones**: Celebrating family milestones, such as birthdays, anniversaries, or achievements, can help reinforce a sense of unity. Including everyone in these celebrations, regardless of biological ties, is key to building a cohesive family unit.

3. **Creating New Rituals**: Developing new rituals that are unique to the blended family can help integrate all members. This could involve creating a family mission statement, planning an annual family trip, or participating in volunteer activities together. These shared experiences help build strong, lasting bonds.

Example of Blending Family Dynamics

An example of blending family dynamics is the story of the Thompson family. When Jane and Robert married, they brought together Jane's two children and Robert's son. Initially, there were struggles with jealousy and competition as the children adjusted to their new family structure. The parents also faced challenges in defining their roles and managing discipline consistently.

However, Jane and Robert focused on open communication and building trust through shared activities. They held regular family meetings to discuss feelings and address any issues that arose. They also created new family traditions, such as a monthly "Thompson Family Day," where they would spend the day together doing something fun and meaningful.

Over time, these efforts paid off. The children began to see each other as true siblings, and the family grew closer. The Thompson family's journey is a testament to the power of patience, communication, and trust in creating a harmonious blended family.

Understanding these dynamics and being proactive in addressing them can help blended families navigate their unique challenges and create a loving, supportive home environment.

FAMILY MOVING
FAMILY

Chapter 3: Preparing for the Transition

The transition to a blended family can be both exciting and challenging for all involved. Preparation is key to ensuring that the transition is as smooth and positive as possible. In this chapter, we'll explore essential steps in preparing for the transition, including communicating with children about the new family structure, setting realistic expectations, and planning and organizing the move.

Communicating with Children About the New Family Structure

One of the most critical aspects of preparing for the transition to a blended family is communicating openly and honestly with your children. How you handle these conversations can significantly impact how they adjust to the changes.

1. **Start Early**: It's important to begin discussing the idea of blending families well before any major changes occur. Children need time to process the information and adjust to the idea of a new family structure. Introducing the concept gradually allows them to ask questions, express their feelings, and begin to adjust mentally and emotionally.
2. **Age-Appropriate Conversations**: Tailor your discussions to the age and maturity level of each child. Younger children may need simpler explanations, focusing on the basics of what will change and reassuring them that they are still loved and secure. Older children and teenagers may have more complex emotions and questions, and they might need more in-depth conversations that address their concerns and involve them in the planning process.
3. **Acknowledge Their Feelings**: Children may experience a range of emotions, from excitement to fear or resentment. It's essential to acknowledge these feelings and validate them. Let your children know that it's okay to feel uncertain or even upset about the changes. Encourage them to share their thoughts and listen to them without

judgment.

4. **Reassure Stability**: One of the biggest fears children may have is the fear of losing their sense of stability. Reassure them that while the family structure is changing, certain things will remain consistent, such as the love and support they receive from you. Emphasize that the new family structure will bring additional people who care for them, rather than taking away from the relationships they already have.

5. **Involve Them in the Process**: Involving children in the process of blending the family can help them feel more in control and less anxious about the changes. This could include letting them have input on living arrangements, such as how their room will be set up, or planning family activities that everyone can enjoy. Giving them a voice in the process helps them feel valued and included.

6. **Addressing Concerns About Loyalty**: Children may feel torn between their biological parents and worry about being disloyal by accepting a stepparent or stepsiblings. It's important to address these concerns directly, reassuring them that they are not betraying their other parent by embracing the new family. Encourage open communication with both biological parents, if possible, to help alleviate these feelings.

Setting Realistic Expectations

Setting realistic expectations is crucial for ensuring a smooth transition to a blended family. Unrealistic expectations can lead to disappointment and frustration, so it's important to approach this new chapter with a clear and balanced perspective.

1. **Understanding the Time Frame**: Blending a family takes time. It's unrealistic to expect that everyone will bond immediately or that the new family unit will function perfectly from the start. Building trust, forming relationships, and creating new routines are processes that can take months or even years. Acknowledge that it's okay if things don't fall into place right away and that patience and perseverance are key.

2. **Avoiding the "Instant Family" Myth**: Popular culture often portrays

blended families as quickly becoming harmonious and close-knit, but the reality is usually more complex. Avoid the expectation that your blended family will immediately feel like a cohesive unit. Relationships will develop at their own pace, and it's important to allow space for this natural progression rather than forcing it.

3. **Expecting Mixed Emotions**: Both adults and children in a blended family may experience a wide range of emotions during the transition. It's important to expect and accept these mixed emotions. Children may have moments of joy and excitement, but they may also experience sadness, anger, or confusion. Similarly, adults may feel overwhelmed at times as they navigate their new roles. Recognizing that these emotions are a normal part of the process can help everyone be more patient and understanding with each other.

4. **Setting Boundaries and Rules Together**: Establishing household rules and boundaries is important, but it's equally important to be realistic about how these will be implemented. Involving children in creating rules can help ensure that they feel respected and heard. However, it's also important to set clear, non-negotiable boundaries to ensure consistency and fairness. Understand that there will likely be some trial and error as the family adjusts to these new rules.

5. **Recognizing That Not All Relationships Will Be the Same**: In a blended family, the relationships between different members will vary. Some stepparents and stepchildren may develop a close bond quickly, while others may take longer or may never form a deep connection. It's important to accept that not all relationships will be the same and that it's okay for each relationship to develop in its own way.

6. **Being Prepared for Challenges**: Challenges are a natural part of blending families. From navigating conflicts between stepsiblings to managing co-parenting dynamics with ex-partners, there will be hurdles to overcome. By setting realistic expectations and being prepared for these challenges, you can approach them with a problem-solving mindset rather than becoming discouraged.

Planning and Organizing the Move

The logistics of moving in together as a blended family can be complex, but careful planning and organization can make the process smoother and less stressful for everyone involved.

1. **Involve the Whole Family**: Moving is a significant event, especially for children. Involve the entire family in the planning process to ensure that everyone feels included and has a say in how things will be organized. This could involve choosing new rooms, deciding how to arrange furniture, or even picking out new items for the home together.

2. **Create a Moving Timeline**: A clear timeline can help manage the move effectively and reduce stress. Start by determining the move-in date and work backward to establish deadlines for packing, arranging transportation, and completing other necessary tasks. Make sure to leave extra time for unexpected delays or complications.

3. **Decluttering and Downsizing**: Before the move, take the opportunity to declutter and downsize belongings. This is particularly important in a blended family where multiple households are coming together. Encourage each family member to sort through their belongings and decide what to keep, donate, or discard. This process can also help reduce feelings of overwhelm and create a fresh start in the new home.

4. **Assigning Responsibilities**: Clearly assign responsibilities for the move to ensure that everyone knows what they need to do. This might include packing certain rooms, organizing transportation, or overseeing the setup of utilities. Giving children age-appropriate tasks can help them feel involved and contribute to the move's success.

5. **Planning the New Living Space**: Consider how the new living space will be organized to accommodate everyone comfortably. If possible, allow each child to have their own space, even if it's just a small area in a shared room. This can help them feel a sense of ownership and security in the new home. Discuss how shared spaces will be used and establish routines for keeping the home organized and tidy.

6. **Managing Emotions During the Move**: Moving can be an emotional time, especially for children who may be leaving behind a familiar

home, neighborhood, or school. Acknowledge these emotions and provide support. Encourage children to say goodbye to the old home in their own way, whether it's through a small farewell gathering or taking pictures to remember it by.

7. **Celebrating the New Beginning**: Once the move is complete, take time to celebrate the new beginning as a family. This could be as simple as a special dinner on the first night in the new home or a small housewarming party. Creating positive memories from the start can help set a hopeful and optimistic tone for your new life together.

Summary

Preparing for the transition to a blended family requires thoughtful communication, realistic expectations, and careful planning. By approaching the process with patience, openness, and a willingness to work through challenges together, you can lay the foundation for a harmonious and loving blended family.

CHAPTER 4
BLENDED FAMILY
NEW
NEW ADVENTURE DAY
SUNDAY ADVENTURE DAY
SUNDAY ADVENTURE DAY
FAMILY MISSION
CHAPTER 4
NEW ADVENTURE DAY
FAMLY MISSION

Chapter 4: Strategies for Smooth Transitions

Successfully blending a family requires more than just moving in together; it demands intentional strategies to foster trust, respect, and a sense of unity among all family members. In this chapter, we'll explore key strategies that can help ease the transition, including building trust and respect, establishing new family traditions, and creating a family mission statement. We'll also share an example of the Johnson family's journey to creating a unified home, illustrating how these strategies can work in real life.

Building Trust and Respect Among Family Members

Trust and respect are the cornerstones of any healthy relationship, and in a blended family, these elements are particularly crucial. The process of building trust and respect requires time, patience, and consistent effort from all family members.

1. **Starting with Small Gestures**: Trust isn't built overnight; it begins with small, everyday actions that demonstrate reliability and care. Simple gestures, such as keeping promises, showing up for important events, and being consistent in your words and actions, can go a long way in establishing trust. For example, if a stepparent promises to attend a child's soccer game, it's important to follow through. These small acts of dependability build a foundation of trust over time.

2. **Open and Honest Communication**: Trust also grows through open and honest communication. Family members should be encouraged to express their thoughts and feelings without fear of judgment or rejection. For instance, if a child is struggling to adjust to a new stepparent, it's important for them to feel safe discussing these feelings. Similarly, stepparents should be open about their own challenges and seek to understand the child's perspective. This mutual sharing helps build trust and respect on both sides.

3. **Respecting Boundaries**: In a blended family, respecting each other's boundaries is essential for building respect. This means acknowledging

and honoring each person's need for personal space, privacy, and time alone. It also involves respecting existing relationships, such as the bond between biological parents and their children, while gradually building new connections. For example, a stepparent should avoid trying to immediately take on the role of a disciplinarian; instead, they should first focus on developing a respectful and trusting relationship with the child.

4. **Empathy and Understanding**: Building trust and respect also involves showing empathy and understanding toward each family member's experience. Blending a family can be emotionally challenging, and each person may have their own fears, insecurities, and hopes. Taking the time to understand and validate these feelings can strengthen the bonds between family members. For instance, acknowledging a child's sense of loss over the changes in their family structure and offering support can help build a deeper sense of trust.

5. **Consistency in Discipline**: Consistency in discipline is another critical factor in building trust and respect. When parents and stepparents present a united front with clear and consistent rules, it fosters a sense of fairness and security. This consistency helps children feel that their environment is predictable and that all adults are working together in their best interests. It's important for parents and stepparents to discuss and agree on discipline strategies to ensure they are applied consistently across the household.

Establishing New Family Traditions

Creating new family traditions is a powerful way to bring a blended family together. These traditions provide a sense of continuity and shared identity, helping family members bond and create lasting memories.

1. **Why Traditions Matter**: Traditions are more than just routine activities; they are rituals that convey meaning, values, and a sense of belonging. For a blended family, establishing new traditions can help bridge the gap between different family backgrounds and create a unified family culture. These traditions can be as simple or elaborate as

you like, but the key is to ensure they are meaningful to all family members.

2. **Starting Simple**: When creating new family traditions, it's often best to start with simple activities that everyone can participate in. For example, you might establish a weekly family game night, where everyone gathers to play board games or watch a movie together. This regular activity can provide a fun and relaxed way for family members to interact and enjoy each other's company.

3. **Incorporating Old Traditions**: While creating new traditions is important, it's also valuable to incorporate elements of old traditions from each side of the blended family. This can help honor the history and identity of each family member. For instance, if one side of the family has a tradition of baking holiday cookies together, this could be incorporated into the new family's holiday celebrations. Blending old and new traditions allows everyone to feel that their background is respected and valued.

4. **Celebrating Milestones**: Establishing traditions around family milestones, such as birthdays, anniversaries, or even the anniversary of when the families first came together, can create a sense of shared history. These celebrations can be an opportunity to reflect on the journey the family has taken together and to reinforce the bonds that have been formed.

5. **Creating New Rituals**: Beyond special occasions, consider creating new daily or weekly rituals that reinforce the family's connection. This might include a bedtime routine where each child shares something they're grateful for, a family dinner where everyone takes turns sharing their highs and lows of the day, or a monthly outing to explore a new place together. These rituals provide a consistent opportunity for connection and help family members feel more united.

6. **Involving Everyone**: It's important that new family traditions reflect the interests and preferences of all family members. Involve everyone in brainstorming ideas for new traditions and make sure that each person feels included in the planning and execution of these activities. This collaborative approach ensures that the traditions are meaningful and enjoyable for everyone.

Creating a Family Mission Statement

A family mission statement is a powerful tool for setting the tone and direction of a blended family. It serves as a guiding principle that reflects the values, goals, and vision of the family as a whole.

1. **What Is a Family Mission Statement?**: A family mission statement is a written declaration of the family's core values, purpose, and goals. It's a statement that captures what the family stands for and what they aim to achieve together. For blended families, a mission statement can help unite everyone under a common purpose and provide clarity during times of conflict or uncertainty.

2. **Involving Everyone in the Process**: Creating a family mission statement should be a collaborative process that involves input from all family members. Start by gathering everyone together to discuss the values that are most important to the family. Encourage each person to share what they believe the family stands for and what they hope to achieve together. This might include values like love, respect, kindness, honesty, or adventure.

3. **Crafting the Statement**: Once everyone has shared their ideas, work together to craft a concise and meaningful statement that encapsulates these values and goals. The mission statement should be short enough to be memorable but comprehensive enough to capture the essence of what the family stands for. For example, the statement might read, "We are a family that supports each other, celebrates our differences, and strives to create a loving, respectful home where everyone feels valued and safe."

4. **Using the Mission Statement**: The family mission statement should be more than just words on paper; it should be a living document that guides the family's actions and decisions. Display the mission statement in a prominent place in the home, such as the living room or kitchen, where everyone can see it regularly. Refer to it when making important decisions or resolving conflicts, using it as a reminder of the family's shared values and goals.

5. **Reviewing and Updating**: As the family grows and evolves, it's

important to periodically review and update the mission statement to ensure it continues to reflect the family's values and goals. Set aside time each year to revisit the statement together and make any necessary adjustments. This process helps keep the family aligned and focused on their shared purpose.

Example: The Johnson Family's Journey to Creating a Unified Home

The Johnson family's journey to blending their families offers a real-life example of how these strategies can be applied to create a unified and loving home.

1. **Background**: When Sarah and Tom Johnson decided to marry, they each brought children from previous marriages into their new union. Sarah had two daughters, Emily and Chloe, while Tom had a son, Jacob. While all three children were excited about the marriage, they also had concerns about how their new family would function.

2. **Building Trust and Respect**: Sarah and Tom knew that building trust and respect among the children was essential. They started by organizing regular family meetings where everyone could share their thoughts and feelings. These meetings provided a safe space for the children to voice their concerns and for Sarah and Tom to listen and respond thoughtfully. Over time, the children began to trust that their opinions mattered and that they were an integral part of the family.

3. **Establishing New Family Traditions**: The Johnsons made it a priority to create new family traditions that would help unite them. One of their favorite traditions became "Sunday Adventure Day," where they would explore a new park, museum, or activity together each week. These outings not only allowed the family to bond over shared experiences but also helped create a sense of excitement and anticipation each week. Additionally, they blended their holiday traditions by incorporating elements from both Sarah's and Tom's families, ensuring that everyone felt represented and included.

4. **Creating a Family Mission Statement**: To further solidify their sense of unity, the Johnsons worked together to create a family mission

statement. They spent an evening discussing what was most important to them as a family, eventually crafting a statement that read, "We are a family that loves unconditionally, supports each other through thick and thin, and celebrates life's journey together." This mission statement became a central part of their home, serving as a reminder of their shared commitment to each other.

5. **Results**: Over time, the Johnson family became a close-knit and supportive unit. While they faced challenges along the way, their commitment to building trust, establishing traditions, and aligning their actions with their mission statement helped them navigate these difficulties with grace. Today, they are a shining example of how intentional strategies can create a harmonious and loving blended family.

Summary

The journey to blending a family is filled with both challenges and opportunities. By focusing on building trust and respect, establishing new family traditions, and creating a family mission statement, you can help ensure a smoother transition and create a unified home. As the Johnson family's story illustrates, these strategies require time, patience, and a commitment to working together, but the rewards of a strong and loving family are well worth the effort.

CO-PARENTING

Chapter 5: Mastering Co-Parenting

Co-parenting in a blended family presents unique challenges and opportunities. Successful co-parenting requires a strong foundation of cooperation, effective communication, and a well-thought-out plan that addresses potential conflicts and disagreements. This chapter delves into the critical aspects of mastering co-parenting, including the importance of cooperation and communication, how to develop a co-parenting plan, strategies for handling conflicts, and an illustrative example of how the Smith family manages their co-parenting relationship.

Importance of Cooperation and Communication

Cooperation and communication are the cornerstones of effective co-parenting. In a blended family, where multiple adults are involved in the upbringing of children, these elements are even more crucial. Cooperation ensures that all parties work together towards the common goal of raising happy, healthy children, while communication facilitates understanding, reduces misunderstandings, and keeps everyone on the same page.

1. **Cooperation**: At its core, cooperation in co-parenting means prioritizing the well-being of the children above all else. This often involves setting aside personal differences and focusing on what is best for the children. In a blended family, cooperation might mean agreeing on consistent rules and expectations across both households, supporting each other's parenting decisions, and working together to provide a stable environment for the children.
    a. For example, if one parent has a rule about bedtime during the school week, it is important that the other parent respects and enforces this rule when the children are in their care. Consistency across households helps children feel secure and understand the boundaries within which they operate.
2. **Communication**: Open and effective communication is essential to making co-parenting work. This means keeping each other informed

about important matters related to the children, such as school events, health issues, or emotional challenges. It also involves discussing and agreeing on parenting strategies, resolving disagreements through dialogue, and ensuring that the children receive clear and consistent messages from both parents.

    a. Good communication requires regular check-ins, whether through phone calls, emails, or in-person meetings, to discuss the children's progress and address any issues that arise. It also means being respectful in all communications, even when there are disagreements, and avoiding using children as messengers between parents.

    b. In blended families, communication extends beyond the biological parents to include stepparents and sometimes other family members, such as grandparents. Everyone involved in the children's upbringing should be part of the communication loop to ensure that everyone is working together effectively.

Developing a Co-Parenting Plan

A co-parenting plan is a vital tool for ensuring that all parties are on the same page and that the needs of the children are met consistently. A well-crafted plan outlines the responsibilities, expectations, and guidelines for both parents, providing a clear framework for how they will work together.

1. **Components of a Co-Parenting Plan**: A comprehensive co-parenting plan should include the following key components:

    a. **Parenting Time and Visitation Schedule**: This section outlines the agreed-upon schedule for when the children will be with each parent. It should include regular visitation times as well as plans for holidays, vacations, and special occasions. Flexibility is important, but having a clear schedule helps to avoid misunderstandings and conflicts.

    b. **Decision-Making Responsibilities**: This component clarifies how major decisions regarding the children's upbringing will be made. This includes decisions related to education, healthcare, religious upbringing, and extracurricular activities. The plan should specify whether decisions will be made jointly or if one parent will have the final say in certain areas.

c. **Communication Guidelines**: This section outlines how and when parents will communicate about the children. It should include preferred methods of communication (e.g., email, phone, in-person meetings) and how often check-ins will occur. It might also include guidelines for how to handle emergency situations or urgent decisions.

d. **Financial Responsibilities**: This component details the financial responsibilities of each parent, including child support, contributions to extracurricular activities, medical expenses, and any other costs related to the children's care. Clear financial arrangements help to prevent conflicts and ensure that all needs are met.

e. **Rules and Discipline**: The plan should include agreed-upon rules and discipline strategies that will be enforced across both households. Consistency in discipline is crucial for providing children with a stable and predictable environment. Parents should agree on core rules (e.g., bedtime, screen time limits, chores) and how discipline will be handled if those rules are broken.

f. **Conflict Resolution**: This section outlines how conflicts between the parents will be resolved. It might include steps for addressing disagreements, such as attempting to resolve the issue through direct communication, seeking mediation, or involving a neutral third party. Having a plan in place for resolving conflicts can help to prevent escalation and keep the focus on the children's best interests.

g. **Involvement of Stepparents and Extended Family**: In a blended family, it's important to clarify the role of stepparents and extended family members in the children's lives. This might include guidelines for how stepparents will be involved in decision-making, discipline, and daily routines, as well as

how communication with extended family members will be
managed.

2. **Reviewing and Updating the Plan**: It's important to regularly review
   and update the co-parenting plan as the children grow and their needs
   change. What works for a toddler might not be suitable for a teenager,
   so the plan should be flexible enough to adapt to changing
   circumstances. Parents should schedule periodic reviews of the plan to
   ensure that it continues to meet the needs of all parties involved.

Handling Conflicts and Disagreements

Conflicts and disagreements are inevitable in any co-parenting relationship, but
how they are handled can make a significant difference in the overall success
of the co-parenting arrangement. It's important to approach conflicts with a
problem-solving mindset, focusing on the best interests of the children rather
than personal grievances.

1. **Keep the Focus on the Children**: When conflicts arise, it's crucial to
   keep the focus on what is best for the children. This means setting aside
   personal differences and working together to find a solution that
   benefits the children's well-being. For example, if there is a
   disagreement about where the children should attend school, both
   parents should consider which option will provide the best education
   and support for the children, rather than insisting on their preference
   out of spite.

2. **Effective Communication During Conflicts**: During disagreements,
   it's important to communicate respectfully and constructively. Avoid
   blaming or accusing language, and instead focus on the issue at hand.
   Use "I" statements to express your concerns (e.g., "I'm concerned about
   how the children will adjust to the new school") and listen actively to
   the other parent's perspective.

3. **Seek Mediation if Necessary**: If a conflict cannot be resolved through
   direct communication, it may be helpful to seek the assistance of a
   mediator. A mediator is a neutral third party who can help facilitate
   discussions and guide the parents toward a mutually acceptable

solution. Mediation can be particularly useful for addressing complex issues or when emotions are running high.

4. **Establishing Boundaries**: Setting clear boundaries can help prevent conflicts from escalating. This might include agreeing not to discuss sensitive issues in front of the children or setting limits on how often and when communication occurs. Boundaries help create a respectful co-parenting relationship and protect the children from being caught in the middle of conflicts.

5. **Agree to Disagree**: In some cases, parents may need to agree to disagree. Not all conflicts will have a perfect solution, and sometimes the best course of action is to accept that there are differences of opinion and move forward with a compromise. The key is to ensure that the resolution, even if imperfect, serves the best interests of the children.

Example: How the Smiths Manage Their Co-Parenting Relationship

The Smith family's co-parenting journey offers valuable insights into how cooperation, communication, and a well-structured plan can lead to successful co-parenting in a blended family.

1. **Background**: When Laura and Mark Smith divorced, they both wanted to ensure that their two children, Anna and Michael, would continue to receive the love and support they needed from both parents. Laura and Mark recognized that despite their differences, they needed to work together to provide a stable and nurturing environment for their children.

2. **Cooperation and Communication**: Laura and Mark made a commitment to maintain open lines of communication and to cooperate on all matters related to the children. They scheduled regular check-ins to discuss Anna and Michael's progress in school, their extracurricular activities, and any behavioral concerns. By staying in regular contact, they were able to address issues quickly and ensure that they were both informed about important aspects of their children's

lives.

3. **Developing a Co-Parenting Plan**: Early on, Laura and Mark worked together to develop a comprehensive co-parenting plan. They agreed on a parenting time schedule that allowed the children to spend ample time with both parents while maintaining consistency in their routines. They also agreed on how to handle major decisions, with both parents having equal input on issues such as education and healthcare.

    a. The plan also included clear guidelines for discipline, with both parents agreeing to enforce the same rules in their respective households. This consistency helped the children feel secure and minimized confusion.

4. **Handling Conflicts and Disagreements**: While Laura and Mark generally got along well, they occasionally faced disagreements, particularly about discipline and extracurricular activities. Rather than letting these disagreements escalate, they used their communication skills to talk through their concerns calmly and respectfully. When they couldn't agree on a solution, they sought the help of a mediator, who helped them find a compromise that worked for both of them.

    a. For example, when they disagreed about whether Anna should join a competitive soccer team that required significant time and financial commitment, they worked with the mediator to explore all options. Ultimately, they decided to allow Anna to join the team but agreed to share the responsibilities and costs associated with it, ensuring that neither parent was overly burdened.

5. **The Outcome**: Through cooperation, effective communication, and a commitment to their co-parenting plan, Laura and Mark have been able to create a stable and supportive environment for Anna and Michael. The children have thrived under this arrangement, maintaining strong relationships with both parents and feeling secure in their blended family structure.

Summary

Mastering co-parenting in a blended family requires dedication, flexibility, and a commitment to putting the children's needs first. By focusing on cooperation and communication, developing a clear and comprehensive co-parenting plan, and approaching conflicts with a problem-solving mindset, parents can create a supportive and nurturing environment for their children. The Smith family's story illustrates that while co-parenting can be challenging, it is possible to build a successful co-parenting relationship that benefits everyone involved.

FAMILY MEETING
CHAPTER
6

Chapter 6: Building Strong Relationships

In a blended family, building strong relationships among all family members is essential for creating a harmonious and loving home. These relationships are the foundation upon which trust, respect, and a sense of unity are built. In this chapter, we will explore strategies for strengthening these bonds, including engaging in bonding activities, encouraging open and honest communication, and supporting each child's individual needs. We will also share an example of how the Williams family used specific activities to foster closeness and create a cohesive family unit.

Bonding Activities for Blended Families

Bonding activities are vital for helping family members in a blended family get to know each other, build trust, and create shared memories. These activities provide opportunities for everyone to connect in a relaxed and enjoyable environment, which can be particularly important during the early stages of blending families.

1. **Family Game Nights**: One of the simplest and most effective bonding activities is a regular family game night. Board games, card games, or even video games that involve multiple players can be a fun way to bring everyone together. Game nights encourage interaction, laughter, and teamwork, which can help break down barriers and build camaraderie among family members. The key is to choose games that everyone can enjoy, regardless of age or skill level.
2. **Outdoor Activities**: Spending time outdoors can be a great way to bond as a family. Activities such as hiking, biking, or going for a picnic provide a chance to explore new environments together and engage in physical activity, which can be both invigorating and stress-relieving. Outdoor adventures can also foster a sense of teamwork as family members navigate trails, set up picnics, or plan activities together.
3. **Cooking and Eating Together**: Preparing and sharing meals as a family is a powerful way to create bonds. Involving everyone in the

cooking process, from planning the menu to chopping vegetables, can make meal preparation a shared experience rather than a chore. This activity encourages collaboration and provides opportunities for conversation and connection. Family meals also create a regular time for everyone to come together and share their day, reinforcing the idea that the family is a supportive unit.

4. **Creative Projects**: Engaging in creative projects together, such as arts and crafts, home improvement projects, or even creating a family scrapbook, can help foster a sense of shared accomplishment. These activities allow family members to express themselves creatively while working toward a common goal. For example, a family might work together to paint and decorate a room in their home, with each person contributing ideas and effort to the final result.

5. **Volunteering as a Family**: Volunteering together can be a meaningful way to bond while giving back to the community. Whether it's participating in a local charity event, helping out at a food bank, or cleaning up a park, volunteering allows family members to work together toward a common cause. This shared experience can create a sense of purpose and unity, reinforcing the family's values and commitment to helping others.

6. **Family Traditions**: Establishing and maintaining family traditions, as discussed in Chapter 4, is another powerful way to build strong relationships. These traditions create continuity and provide regular opportunities for the family to come together in meaningful ways. Whether it's an annual holiday celebration, a monthly movie night, or a special ritual before bedtime, traditions help anchor the family and create lasting memories.

Encouraging Open and Honest Communication

Communication is the lifeblood of any relationship, and in a blended family, it's particularly important to encourage open and honest dialogue. Effective communication fosters understanding, builds trust, and helps resolve conflicts before they escalate.

1. **Creating a Safe Environment for Expression**: One of the most important aspects of encouraging open communication is creating an environment where everyone feels safe expressing their thoughts and feelings. Family members, especially children, should know that their opinions are valued and that they can speak up without fear of judgment or punishment. This can be achieved by actively listening to each other, validating emotions, and responding with empathy.

2. **Regular Family Meetings**: Holding regular family meetings is a practical way to ensure that everyone has a voice. These meetings can be scheduled weekly or monthly and provide a structured time for family members to discuss issues, plan activities, and share updates. During these meetings, it's important to create a space where everyone, from the youngest to the oldest, feels comfortable contributing. Encourage each person to share something positive, voice any concerns, and suggest ideas for family activities.

3. **One-on-One Time**: While group communication is important, one-on-one conversations between parents and children or between stepparents and stepchildren can also be incredibly valuable. These private discussions allow for more intimate, focused communication and can help strengthen individual relationships within the family. Scheduling regular one-on-one time with each child, such as a weekly outing or a quiet chat before bedtime, can make a significant difference in building trust and understanding.

4. **Addressing Issues Promptly**: In a blended family, it's crucial to address issues as they arise rather than letting them fester. When conflicts or misunderstandings occur, they should be discussed openly and resolved quickly to prevent resentment from building. Parents should model healthy communication by addressing their disagreements calmly and respectfully, demonstrating to children that conflicts can be resolved through dialogue rather than arguments.

5. **Encouraging Emotional Literacy**: Teaching children to identify and articulate their emotions can greatly enhance communication within the family. Encourage children to express how they feel, whether they are happy, sad, frustrated, or excited, and help them understand that all emotions are valid. By fostering emotional literacy, parents can help

children communicate more effectively and reduce the likelihood of emotional outbursts or misunderstandings.

6. **Being Transparent About Family Dynamics**: In blended families, it's important to be transparent about the unique dynamics at play. This includes discussing the roles of stepparents, the relationships between stepsiblings, and any ongoing connections with biological parents outside the household. Openly acknowledging these dynamics helps prevent confusion and ensures that everyone is clear about their place within the family structure.

Supporting Each Child's Individual Needs

In a blended family, it's essential to recognize and support the individual needs of each child. While building strong family bonds is important, it's equally crucial to ensure that each child feels seen, heard, and valued as an individual.

1. **Recognizing Individual Differences**: Each child in a blended family brings their own personality, interests, and experiences to the table. It's important for parents and stepparents to recognize and celebrate these differences. This might involve acknowledging a child's unique hobbies, supporting their academic or extracurricular interests, or simply making time to listen to their individual concerns. By showing that you appreciate and respect each child's individuality, you help them feel secure and valued within the family.

2. **Providing Personalized Attention**: While it's important to spend time together as a family, it's also vital to provide personalized attention to each child. This can be as simple as setting aside time each week for one-on-one activities, such as going for a walk, playing a game, or having a private conversation. These moments of individual attention help strengthen the parent-child or stepparent-child bond and ensure that each child feels special and important.

3. **Supporting Emotional Needs**: Children in blended families may have a range of emotions about the changes in their family structure. Some may feel excited, while others may experience feelings of loss, confusion, or jealousy. It's important for parents to be attuned to these

emotional needs and to provide the necessary support. This might involve talking through difficult feelings, seeking professional counseling if needed, or simply being there to listen and offer reassurance.

4. **Encouraging Independence**: Supporting each child's individual needs also involves encouraging their independence and personal growth. This can be done by giving them responsibilities that match their age and abilities, encouraging them to pursue their interests, and supporting their efforts to develop their own identity. For example, if a child expresses interest in a new hobby or sport, parents should do their best to provide the resources and encouragement needed for the child to explore that interest.

5. **Creating an Inclusive Environment**: It's important to create an environment where all children, regardless of whether they are biological or stepchildren, feel equally included and important. This means being mindful of favoritism and ensuring that all children have a voice in family decisions and activities. Parents should strive to treat all children fairly and to provide equal opportunities for attention, love, and support.

6. **Being Patient and Understanding**: Supporting each child's individual needs requires patience and understanding, particularly as children adjust to the new family dynamics. Some children may take longer to warm up to stepparents or stepsiblings, and that's okay. It's important to give them the time and space they need to adjust at their own pace, while also providing consistent love and support.

Example: Activities That Helped the Williams Family Bond

The Williams family's experience offers a practical example of how bonding activities, communication, and individual support can help a blended family come together.

1. **Background**: When Jane and Robert Williams married, they each brought children from previous marriages into their new family. Jane

had two sons, David and Chris, while Robert had a daughter, Emma. Initially, the children were hesitant about the new family arrangement, and there were moments of tension and uncertainty.

2. **Bonding Activities**: To help the family bond, Jane and Robert decided to introduce regular family game nights. Every Friday evening, the family would gather to play board games or watch a movie together. This weekly tradition became something the children looked forward to and provided a relaxed setting where they could interact and have fun without the pressures of day-to-day life.

    a. In addition to game nights, the Williams family also started taking weekend hikes together. These outdoor adventures allowed the family to spend time in nature, working together to navigate trails and enjoy the beauty of their surroundings. These hikes became an opportunity for the family to connect, share stories, and support each other, strengthening their bonds over time.

3. **Encouraging Open Communication**: Jane and Robert understood the importance of communication and made it a point to hold family meetings once a week. During these meetings, everyone had the chance to share their thoughts and feelings about how things were going. The meetings were a safe space for discussing any issues, planning future activities, and celebrating achievements.

    a. Jane and Robert also made an effort to spend one-on-one time with each child. For example, Robert would take Emma out for breakfast every Saturday morning, while Jane would go on walks with David and Chris individually. These one-on-one interactions allowed the children to feel valued and understood, helping to build strong individual relationships.

4. **Supporting Individual Needs**: Jane and Robert recognized that each child had their own unique needs and interests. David was passionate about soccer, so they made sure he had the opportunity to join a local soccer team and attend practices regularly. Chris was more academically inclined, so they supported his interest in science by helping him set up a small lab space in the garage. Emma loved music, so they enrolled her in piano lessons and attended her recitals to show

their support.

    a. By taking the time to understand and support each child's interests, Jane and Robert helped the children feel more secure and confident in their new family environment.

5. **The Outcome**: Over time, the Williams family grew closer, with each member feeling more comfortable and connected. The combination of bonding activities, open communication, and individualized support helped create a strong and loving family unit. While there were still challenges along the way, the foundation they built through these efforts allowed them to face those challenges together as a united family.

Summary

Building strong relationships in a blended family requires a thoughtful approach that includes engaging in bonding activities, encouraging open and honest communication, and supporting each child's individual needs. By implementing these strategies, families can create a supportive and loving environment where all members feel valued and connected. The Williams family's experience demonstrates that with patience, effort, and a commitment to each other, blended families can successfully navigate the complexities of their new dynamics and emerge stronger together.

Emotion Coaching
Journaling
Encouraging Empathy
Positive Reinforcement
Open Communication
Recognizing The Signs
Chapter 7

Chapter 7: Addressing Common Challenges

Blending a family can be a rewarding experience, but it also comes with its share of challenges. Understanding and addressing these challenges is crucial to building a cohesive and loving family unit. In this chapter, we'll delve into some of the most common issues faced by blended families, including managing jealousy and competition, dealing with ex-partners and external influences, and overcoming financial and logistical issues. We will also share an example of how the Taylor family faced and overcame these challenges.

Managing Jealousy and Competition

Jealousy and competition are natural emotions that can arise in a blended family, especially among children who suddenly find themselves sharing their parents' attention with new siblings. These feelings, if not addressed, can lead to resentment and conflict within the family.

1. **Recognizing the Signs**: The first step in managing jealousy and competition is recognizing the signs. Children may express their feelings in various ways, such as through sibling rivalry, withdrawal, or acting out. They might compete for attention, trying to outdo one another in areas like school performance, sports, or chores. It's important for parents to be attuned to these behaviors and to understand that they often stem from feelings of insecurity or fear of losing their place in the family.

2. **Open Communication**: Encouraging open communication about these feelings is essential. Create a safe space where children feel comfortable expressing their emotions without fear of judgment. Let them know that it's okay to feel jealous or competitive and that these feelings are normal. Parents should listen empathetically, acknowledging the child's feelings and reassuring them of their unique place in the family. For example, a parent might say, "I understand that it's hard to share attention, but you are just as important and loved as everyone else."

Open Communication Techniques for Managing Jealousy and Competition

Open communication is vital in managing jealousy and competition within a blended family. Creating an environment where all family members feel heard and understood can significantly reduce tension and help foster a more harmonious household. Below are some suggested techniques to encourage open communication and address jealousy and competition effectively.

1. Family Meetings

One effective way to promote open communication is through regular family meetings. These meetings provide a structured opportunity for everyone to share their thoughts, concerns, and feelings in a safe and supportive environment. During these meetings, each family member should have the chance to speak without interruption. This not only helps to identify any issues related to jealousy or competition but also encourages everyone to participate in finding solutions.

Technique: Establish a regular time for family meetings, such as once a week or once a month. Start each meeting with a positive activity, like sharing something good that happened during the week, to set a constructive tone. Then, move on to discussing any concerns or issues. Encourage the children to share how they feel about their relationships with siblings and parents, and brainstorm ways to address any negative feelings.

2. Active Listening

Active listening is a powerful tool in fostering open communication. When family members feel truly listened to, they are more likely to express their feelings honestly and less likely to harbor resentment. Active listening involves giving full attention to the speaker, acknowledging their emotions, and responding thoughtfully without immediately offering solutions or judgments.

Technique: When a child expresses feelings of jealousy or competition, practice active listening by making eye contact, nodding, and using phrases like "I understand that you're feeling…". Reflect back what the child has said to ensure you've understood their feelings correctly, such as "It sounds like you're upset because you feel like you're not getting enough attention." This approach validates the child's emotions and opens the door to deeper, more meaningful conversations.

3. Emotion Coaching

Emotion coaching involves helping children understand and articulate their emotions. In a blended family, children may struggle to identify or express feelings of jealousy or insecurity, leading to behavioral issues. By coaching them through their emotions, parents can help children process their feelings in a healthy way and reduce the impact of jealousy on family dynamics.

Technique: When a child is acting out or showing signs of jealousy, take a moment to sit with them and help them identify what they're feeling. For example, you might say, "I notice that you're upset whenever your stepbrother gets praise. Do you think you might be feeling jealous?" Once the emotion is identified, help the child find constructive ways to deal with it, such as talking about it openly or finding ways to feel more secure in their own accomplishments.

4. Journaling

Encouraging children to keep a journal can be an effective way for them to express their feelings in a private and reflective way. Writing down their thoughts can help children process their emotions and gain clarity on what's bothering them. This can be particularly useful for children who might find it difficult to verbalize their feelings in family meetings or one-on-one conversations.

Technique: Provide each child with a journal and encourage them to write in it regularly. You might suggest specific prompts, such as "What made you feel happy today?" or "Is there something that made you feel left out?" Journaling can also be a springboard for further discussion; if the child feels comfortable, they can share parts of their journal with you to talk through any issues they've written about.

5. Role-Playing

Role-playing can be a helpful technique for exploring and addressing jealousy and competition in a safe, controlled environment. By acting out different scenarios, children can gain insight into how their actions and words affect others, and they can practice responding to situations in positive ways.

Technique: Set up a role-playing session where you and the children act out a common scenario that triggers jealousy or competition, such as one child receiving praise while another does not. After the role-play, discuss how each person felt during the scenario and explore alternative ways to handle the situation. This technique can be particularly effective in helping children develop empathy and understanding for their siblings.

6. Encouraging Empathy

Building empathy among siblings is crucial in reducing feelings of jealousy and competition. When children learn to understand and appreciate each other's perspectives, they are more likely to support one another rather than compete.

Technique: Encourage empathy by helping children see situations from their siblings' point of view. For example, if one child is jealous because their sibling received a special reward, ask them to consider how their sibling might feel in that situation and why they received the reward. You could say, "How do you think your brother felt when he got that award? He worked hard on that project. What do you think you might have done differently if you were in his place?" This helps children develop a deeper understanding of each other's experiences and emotions.

7. Positive Reinforcement

Positive reinforcement can be a powerful motivator in managing jealousy and competition. Recognizing and rewarding positive behavior, such as cooperation, sharing, or supporting a sibling, can encourage more of the same behavior.

Technique: Whenever you notice a child displaying a positive behavior, such as helping a sibling or celebrating their sibling's success, acknowledge it immediately with praise. You might say, "I really appreciate how you helped your sister with her homework today. That was very kind of you." Consistent positive reinforcement helps to shift the focus from competition to cooperation and mutual support within the family.

Summary

Open communication is a key strategy in managing jealousy and competition in a blended family. By implementing these techniques—such as holding family meetings, practicing active listening, coaching emotions, encouraging journaling, role-playing, fostering empathy, and using positive reinforcement—parents can create an environment where all family members feel heard, understood, and valued. This approach not only helps to address feelings of jealousy but also strengthens the overall bonds within the family, promoting a sense of unity and mutual respect.

1. **Avoiding Favoritism**: In a blended family, avoiding favoritism is crucial to maintaining harmony and preventing jealousy and competition among siblings. Favoritism, whether real or perceived, can lead to feelings of resentment, insecurity, and division within the family. To foster a sense of fairness and inclusivity, parents must be mindful of how they interact with each child and take steps to ensure that each one feels equally valued and loved. Below are some suggested techniques for avoiding favoritism in a blended family.

Techniques To Avoid Favoritism

1. Equal Attention and Praise

One of the most important ways to avoid favoritism is by giving equal attention and praise to all children. Every child needs to feel recognized and appreciated for their unique strengths and accomplishments. This doesn't mean that every child must receive the same amount of attention at all times, but over time, the distribution of attention and praise should feel balanced.

Technique: Make a conscious effort to acknowledge and celebrate each child's achievements, no matter how small. For example, if one child excels academically and another is more artistic, praise each child for their respective talents. You might say, "I'm so proud of your grades—great job!" to one child, and "Your painting is beautiful—I love how creative you are!" to the other. By recognizing each child's individuality, you reinforce the idea that every member of the family is valued.

2. Rotate Responsibilities and Privileges

In a blended family, it's important to ensure that responsibilities and privileges are shared fairly among all children. If one child consistently gets the "best" chores or the most favorable privileges, it can create feelings of favoritism and resentment. Rotating these duties and privileges helps to ensure that no child feels left out or unfairly treated.

Technique: Create a rotating schedule for chores and privileges. For example, if you have a weekly family movie night, rotate who gets to choose the movie. Similarly, if one child has the privilege of sitting in the front seat of the car, rotate this privilege among all the children. By sharing these responsibilities and privileges, you demonstrate fairness and reduce the likelihood of jealousy.

3. Avoiding Comparisons

Comparing siblings, even in subtle ways, can lead to feelings of inadequacy and competition. It's essential to treat each child as an individual with their own unique strengths and challenges, rather than comparing them to one another.

Technique: Be mindful of your language when talking to your children. Instead of saying things like, "Why can't you be more like your sister?" focus on each child's individual progress and growth. For example, say, "I'm really proud of how hard you're working on your math homework. Keep it up!" This approach avoids creating a sense of competition and helps each child feel valued for who they are.

4. Inclusive Family Activities

Favoritism can sometimes manifest in the types of activities parents choose to engage in with their children. To avoid this, it's important to plan family activities that are inclusive and enjoyable for all members, rather than focusing on activities that only appeal to one child's interests.

Technique: When planning family outings or activities, consider each child's interests and try to find activities that everyone can enjoy. For instance, if one child loves sports and another prefers art, plan a day that includes both a trip to a local park for a game and a visit to an art museum. By including elements that appeal to each child, you show that everyone's interests are important and valued.

5. Consistent Rules and Discipline

Consistency in rules and discipline is key to avoiding perceptions of favoritism. If children see that rules are applied differently to different siblings, they may feel that one child is favored over the others. Consistent enforcement of rules helps to create a sense of fairness and security.

Technique: Establish clear and consistent rules for the household that apply to all children equally. If a rule is broken, ensure that the consequences are the same for everyone, regardless of age or gender. For example, if the rule is that screen time is limited to one hour per day, this should apply to all children. If one child breaks the rule, the same consequence should be applied as it would be for any other child. Consistency in discipline helps reinforce that all children are held to the same standards, which reduces feelings of favoritism.

6. Spending Quality Time with Each Child

In a blended family, it's essential to spend quality one-on-one time with each child to reinforce their unique bond with you. This time should be focused on the child's interests and needs, helping them feel special and valued as an individual.

Technique: Schedule regular one-on-one activities with each child. These could be simple outings like going for ice cream, taking a walk, or engaging in a hobby they enjoy. The goal is to make each child feel that they have your undivided attention and that their relationship with you is important. For example, if one child loves reading, you might spend an afternoon together at a bookstore or library. By making time for each child individually, you demonstrate that each relationship is unique and equally valued.

7. Seek Feedback from Your Children

Sometimes, parents may not be aware of how their actions are perceived by their children. Seeking feedback from your children can help you identify any unintentional favoritism and take steps to address it.

Technique: Have open conversations with your children about how they feel in the family dynamic. You might ask questions like, "Do you feel that I spend enough time with you?" or "Is there anything you wish was different about how we do things as a family?" Listening to their feedback can help you adjust your approach and ensure that each child feels equally loved and supported.

Summary

Avoiding favoritism is essential for fostering a sense of fairness and unity in a blended family. By implementing these techniques—such as giving equal attention and praise, rotating responsibilities, avoiding comparisons, planning inclusive activities, applying consistent discipline, spending quality time with each child, and seeking feedback—you can help ensure that all children feel equally valued and loved. This approach not only reduces feelings of jealousy and competition but also strengthens the bonds within the family, creating a more harmonious and supportive environment for everyone.

1. **Encouraging Teamwork**: Fostering a sense of teamwork among siblings can help reduce competition and promote unity. Encourage activities that require cooperation rather than competition, such as group projects, family games that require collaboration, or household tasks where siblings work together. By shifting the focus from individual success to group success, children can learn to appreciate

each other's strengths and support one another.

2. **One-on-One Time**: Spending one-on-one time with each child is crucial in addressing jealousy. This helps ensure that each child feels special and valued. Parents should make a regular effort to carve out time for individual activities with each child, whether it's a trip to the park, a special outing, or simply a quiet conversation. This focused attention can help mitigate feelings of jealousy and reinforce each child's sense of security and belonging.

Dealing with Ex-Partners and External Influences

In a blended family, dealing with ex-partners and external influences, such as extended family members or friends, can present significant challenges. These external factors can impact the dynamics within the blended family, sometimes causing tension or conflict.

1. **Establishing Boundaries**: Establishing clear boundaries with ex-partners is essential for maintaining a peaceful co-parenting relationship and protecting the blended family's unity. Boundaries might include guidelines for communication, such as agreeing to discuss only issues related to the children and to do so in a respectful manner. It's also important to set boundaries around involvement in the new family's daily life, ensuring that ex-partners respect the space and privacy of the new family unit.

2. **Consistent Co-Parenting**: Consistency in co-parenting between households is key to reducing conflict and confusion for the children. Parents should work together to create a co-parenting plan that outlines shared responsibilities, rules, and expectations. This plan should be communicated clearly to the children so they understand what is expected of them in both households. When parents present a united front, even across separate households, it provides stability and security for the children.

3. **Handling Negative Influence**: Sometimes, ex-partners or external family members may try to undermine the blended family's unity, whether intentionally or unintentionally. This could manifest as

criticism of the new stepparent, negative comments about the blended family, or attempts to influence the children's attitudes. In these cases, it's important to address the issue directly and assertively. Parents should have a private conversation with the ex-partner or family member to express concerns and request that they respect the boundaries of the new family. Children should also be reassured that they can express their feelings openly, and any negative comments they hear should be countered with positive reinforcement of the family's values and goals.

4. **Maintaining a Positive Relationship**: While it can be challenging, maintaining a positive relationship with an ex-partner is beneficial for the children and the blended family as a whole. This doesn't mean becoming best friends, but it does mean being civil, cooperative, and respectful in all interactions. When children see that their parents can work together amicably, it reduces their stress and anxiety, making it easier for them to adjust to the blended family dynamic.

5. **Managing Expectations with Extended Family**: External influences aren't limited to ex-partners; extended family members, such as grandparents, aunts, and uncles, can also impact the blended family. It's important to communicate expectations clearly with extended family members, especially if they are accustomed to the way things were before the new family was formed. This might involve having conversations about how holidays will be spent, how much involvement they will have in the children's lives, and what role they will play in the new family structure. By setting these expectations early on, parents can help prevent misunderstandings and ensure that extended family members support rather than hinder the blended family's growth.

Overcoming Financial and Logistical Issues

Financial and logistical issues are common challenges in blended families, particularly when multiple households are merging or when parents have different financial habits or obligations. Addressing these challenges requires careful planning, clear communication, and a willingness to work together.

1. **Creating a Family Budget**: One of the first steps in overcoming financial challenges is creating a family budget. This budget should take into account all sources of income, as well as all expenses, including those related to the children, such as school fees, extracurricular activities, and healthcare costs. It's important to be transparent about financial obligations, including any child support payments or debts that may impact the family's finances. By working together to create a realistic budget, parents can ensure that all needs are met and that financial stress is minimized.

2. **Discussing Financial Priorities**: In a blended family, parents may have different financial priorities or philosophies. It's crucial to have open and honest discussions about these priorities to avoid conflicts down the line. For example, one parent might prioritize saving for the children's college education, while the other might focus on paying off debt. By discussing these priorities and finding a compromise, parents can align their financial goals and work together to achieve them.

3. **Managing Logistical Challenges**: Logistical challenges, such as coordinating schedules, transportation, and childcare, are common in blended families. These challenges can be exacerbated if parents live in different locations or if the children have busy extracurricular schedules. To manage these logistics effectively, parents should use tools such as shared calendars or family planning apps to keep track of everyone's schedules. Regular family meetings can also help ensure that everyone is on the same page and that any potential conflicts are addressed in advance.

4. **Planning for Unexpected Expenses**: Unexpected expenses can arise in any family, but they can be particularly challenging in a blended family where financial obligations may already be stretched. It's important to build an emergency fund to cover unexpected costs, such as medical bills or car repairs. This fund provides a financial cushion that can prevent these expenses from causing stress or conflict within the family.

5. **Sharing Responsibilities**: In addition to financial responsibilities, logistical responsibilities, such as household chores, transportation, and meal planning, should also be shared among family members. Dividing these tasks fairly can help prevent one parent from becoming

overwhelmed and can also teach children valuable life skills. For example, older children might take on responsibilities such as helping with younger siblings or preparing simple meals, while parents share the tasks of driving to and from activities or managing household finances.

6. **Seeking Professional Advice**: In some cases, blended families may benefit from seeking professional financial advice. A financial planner can help parents navigate complex financial situations, such as merging assets, managing child support, or planning for the future. By seeking professional advice, parents can gain clarity on their financial situation and develop a plan that meets the needs of the entire family.

Example: The Challenges Faced by the Taylor Family and How They Overcame Them

The Taylor family's experience illustrates how blended families can successfully navigate common challenges with communication, planning, and a commitment to working together.

1. **Background**: When Sarah and James Taylor married, they each brought two children from previous marriages into their new family. Sarah's daughters, Emma and Lily, were used to being the center of attention, while James's sons, Jack and Ryan, were more independent. The blending of these two families brought about a range of challenges, from sibling rivalry to financial and logistical issues.

2. **Managing Jealousy and Competition**: Emma and Lily initially struggled with jealousy and competition, feeling that they had to compete with their new stepbrothers for their mother's attention. Sarah and James recognized this early on and made a concerted effort to spend one-on-one time with each child. Sarah took Emma and Lily on special outings, while James did the same with Jack and Ryan. They also introduced family game nights, where everyone could participate and enjoy time together, helping to reduce competition and foster a sense of unity.

3. **Dealing with Ex-Partners and External Influences**: Both Sarah and

James had ex-partners who were still actively involved in their children's lives. To manage this, they established clear boundaries and communication guidelines with their ex-partners. They agreed that all communication would be focused on the children's needs and that any issues would be discussed privately, away from the children. This approach helped to reduce tension and allowed the Taylor family to build a strong, united front.

4. **Overcoming Financial and Logistical Issues**: Financially, merging two households was a challenge. Sarah and James sat down together to create a detailed budget that included all of their income and expenses. They also set up a joint account for shared household expenses while maintaining separate accounts for personal spending. Logistically, they used a shared online calendar to keep track of the children's schedules, including school events, extracurricular activities, and visitation times with their other parents. By staying organized and communicating regularly, they were able to manage the complexities of their blended family life.

5. **The Outcome**: Over time, the Taylor family grew closer and more cohesive. By addressing jealousy, setting boundaries with ex-partners, and carefully managing their finances and schedules, Sarah and James were able to create a stable and loving environment for their children. While challenges still arose from time to time, they had developed the tools and strategies needed to navigate them successfully, ensuring that their blended family continued to thrive.

Summary

Avoiding favoritism is essential for fostering a sense of fairness and unity in a blended family. By implementing these techniques—such as giving equal attention and praise, rotating responsibilities, avoiding comparisons, planning inclusive activities, applying consistent discipline, spending quality time with each child, and seeking feedback—you can help ensure that all children feel equally valued and loved. This approach not only reduces feelings of jealousy and competition but also strengthens the bonds within the family, creating a more harmonious and supportive environment for everyone.

Chapter 8: Celebrating Diversity and Unity

Blended families often bring together individuals from diverse backgrounds, cultures, and traditions. While this diversity can present challenges, it also offers a unique opportunity to enrich the family experience by embracing and celebrating these differences. In this chapter, we will explore the importance of embracing different backgrounds and cultures, encouraging mutual respect and understanding, and celebrating family milestones and achievements. We'll also share an example of how the Garcia family used multicultural celebrations to foster unity within their blended family.

Embracing Different Backgrounds and Cultures

In a blended family, members may come from different cultural, ethnic, or religious backgrounds, each bringing their own traditions, values, and perspectives. Embracing these differences can strengthen the family by creating a richer, more inclusive environment.

Understanding Each Other's Backgrounds: The first step in embracing different backgrounds and cultures is gaining a deep understanding of each other's heritage. This involves learning about each family member's cultural practices, traditions, and values. Taking the time to ask questions, listen, and show genuine interest in each other's backgrounds helps to build a foundation of mutual respect.

Technique: Encourage family members to share stories about their heritage, family traditions, and cultural practices. You might have a "culture night" where each member of the family presents something unique from their background, such as a traditional dish, a holiday custom, or a special song. This not only helps everyone learn more about each other but also creates a sense of pride and connection to one's roots.

Incorporating Cultural Traditions into Family Life: Once you have an understanding of each other's backgrounds, the next step is to incorporate

these cultural traditions into your family's daily life. This could involve celebrating holidays from different cultures, cooking traditional meals together, or practicing religious or spiritual rituals as a family. By integrating these practices into your routine, you create a family culture that honors and respects each member's heritage.

Technique: Create a family calendar that includes important cultural holidays and events from each member's background. Make a point to celebrate these occasions together, perhaps by cooking a traditional meal, participating in a cultural activity, or learning more about the significance of the holiday. This not only educates the family about different cultures but also reinforces the idea that each person's heritage is valued and respected.

Blending New Traditions: While it's important to honor existing cultural traditions, blended families also have the opportunity to create new traditions that reflect the diversity of the family. These new traditions can serve as a symbol of the family's unity and shared values, combining elements from each member's background to create something unique and meaningful.

Technique: Work together as a family to develop new traditions that blend different cultural practices. For example, you might create a new holiday tradition that incorporates elements from various cultures, such as exchanging gifts on a specific day or preparing a meal that includes dishes from different countries. These new traditions can help solidify the family's identity while celebrating the diversity within it.

Encouraging Mutual Respect and Understanding

Mutual respect and understanding are essential for fostering a harmonious blended family, especially when family members come from diverse backgrounds. Encouraging these values helps to build trust, reduce conflict, and create a supportive environment where everyone feels valued.

1. **Open Dialogue About Differences:** Encouraging open dialogue

about cultural differences is key to building mutual respect. Family members should feel comfortable discussing their beliefs, traditions, and values without fear of judgment or misunderstanding. These conversations provide an opportunity to dispel stereotypes, address misconceptions, and foster a deeper understanding of each other.

    a. **Technique:** Facilitate regular family discussions where members can share their thoughts and experiences related to culture and identity. Create a safe space where everyone feels heard and respected. For example, you might hold a monthly family meeting where a different family member leads a discussion about a particular cultural practice or belief. This approach not only promotes understanding but also strengthens the family's bonds.

2. **Modeling Respectful Behavior:** Parents and stepparents play a crucial role in modeling respectful behavior. Children often learn how to interact with others by observing the adults in their lives. By demonstrating respect for each other's backgrounds and traditions, parents set a positive example for their children to follow.

    a. **Technique:** Show respect for your partner's cultural practices, even if they are different from your own. This might involve participating in cultural traditions that are new to you or expressing interest in learning more about your partner's heritage. When children see their parents engaging with each other's cultures in a positive and respectful way, they are more likely to adopt the same attitude.

3. **Addressing Conflicts Constructively:** In a blended family, cultural differences can sometimes lead to misunderstandings or conflicts. It's important to address these issues constructively, with a focus on finding common ground and maintaining respect. Conflict resolution should involve open communication, empathy, and a willingness to compromise.

    a. **Technique:** When a conflict arises due to cultural differences, approach the situation with curiosity rather than defensiveness. Ask questions to understand the other person's perspective, and express your own views calmly and respectfully. For example, if there is a disagreement about how to celebrate a holiday, discuss each person's expectations and find a compromise that honors both perspectives. This approach helps to resolve conflicts in a way that strengthens, rather than weakens, family relationships.

Celebrating Family Milestones and Achievements

Celebrating family milestones and achievements is a powerful way to foster unity and reinforce the bonds within a blended family. These celebrations provide an opportunity to recognize each member's contributions and to create shared memories that strengthen the family's identity.

1. **Recognizing Individual Achievements:** It's important to celebrate the achievements of each family member, whether they are academic, athletic, personal, or professional. Recognizing individual accomplishments shows that each person's efforts are valued and appreciated, and it helps to build self-esteem and confidence.
    a. **Technique:** Create a family tradition of celebrating individual achievements with a special dinner, a family outing, or a small ceremony. For example, if a child excels in school or sports, the family might go out for ice cream to celebrate, or the parents might present the child with a certificate of achievement. These celebrations help to reinforce the idea that each person's successes contribute to the overall strength and happiness of the family.
2. **Celebrating Collective Milestones:** In addition to individual achievements, it's important to celebrate milestones that involve the entire family. This could include anniversaries, the completion of a family project, or the achievement of a collective goal, such as saving for a family vacation or completing a home renovation.
    a. **Technique:** Mark family milestones with special celebrations that involve all members. For example, you might throw a family party to celebrate the anniversary of the day your blended family came together or plan a special trip to

commemorate a significant achievement. These collective celebrations help to create a sense of shared history and reinforce the family's unity.

3. **Creating Lasting Memories:** Celebrating milestones and achievements is not just about the event itself, but also about creating lasting memories that the family can cherish for years to come. These memories help to build a strong sense of identity and belonging within the family.

    a. **Technique**: Document family celebrations with photos, videos, or a family scrapbook. After each celebration, take the time to reflect on the experience as a family, perhaps by sharing favorite moments or writing about the event in a family journal. These practices help to preserve the memories of special occasions and create a tangible record of the family's journey together.

Example: The Garcia Family's Multicultural Celebrations

The Garcia family provides a wonderful example of how a blended family can embrace diversity and unity through multicultural celebrations.

1. **Background:** When Maria and Carlos Garcia married, they brought together two families from different cultural backgrounds. Maria's heritage was rooted in Mexican traditions, while Carlos came from a Filipino background. They wanted to ensure that their blended family honored and celebrated both cultures, while also creating new traditions that reflected their shared values.

2. **Embracing Cultural Traditions:** From the beginning, Maria and Carlos made a point of incorporating both Mexican and Filipino traditions into their family life. They celebrated Mexican holidays such as Día de los Muertos and Mexican Independence Day, as well as Filipino festivals like Simbang Gabi and Araw ng Kalayaan. These celebrations often involved preparing traditional foods, decorating the house with cultural symbols, and participating in community events.

3. **Encouraging Mutual Respect and Understanding:** To help their children appreciate both cultures, Maria and Carlos facilitated open discussions about the significance of each tradition. They encouraged their children to ask questions and share their thoughts about what the traditions meant to them. These conversations helped the children develop a deeper understanding and respect for both sides of their heritage.

4. **Creating New Traditions:** The Garcia family also created new traditions that blended elements from both cultures. For example, they combined the Mexican custom of Las Posadas with the Filipino tradition of Noche Buena to create a unique holiday celebration that included elements from both backgrounds. They also started a new tradition of family storytelling, where each family member would share stories from their cultural heritage during special gatherings.

5. **Celebrating Milestones:** The Garcias made it a point to celebrate both individual and collective milestones. When their daughter Sofia won an academic award, the family held a special dinner in her honor, incorporating her favorite dishes from both Mexican and Filipino cuisine. They also celebrated their fifth wedding anniversary with a family trip to the Philippines, where they explored Carlos's heritage and created lasting memories together.

6. **The Outcome:** Through their commitment to embracing diversity and unity, the Garcia family created a rich and inclusive family culture that honored both Mexican and Filipino traditions. Their multicultural celebrations became a source of pride and connection for all family members, reinforcing the bonds within their blended family and creating a strong sense of identity and belonging.

Summary

Celebrating diversity and unity is essential for creating a harmonious and inclusive environment in a blended family. By embracing different backgrounds and cultures, encouraging mutual respect and understanding, and celebrating family milestones and achievements, families can build strong bonds that honor each member's heritage while creating a shared sense of identity. The Garcia family's experience illustrates the power of multicultural celebrations in fostering unity and enriching the family experience, showing that when diversity is embraced, it can become a source of strength and pride for the entire family.

Conclusion

Blending a family is a journey filled with both challenges and rewards. As we've explored throughout this book, the process of creating a harmonious and loving blended family requires intentional effort, patience, and a deep commitment to understanding and supporting each family member. As we conclude this journey together, let's recap the key points discussed, offer encouragement for the road ahead, and provide additional resources for ongoing support and information.

Recap of Key Points

1. **Understanding Blended Families:** We began by defining what it means to be a blended family and exploring the various dynamics that come with merging different family units. Understanding the complexities of these dynamics is essential to navigating the unique challenges that blended families face.

2. **Preparing for the Transition:** Preparation is crucial when bringing together families with different backgrounds, expectations, and routines. Communicating openly with children about the new family structure, setting realistic expectations, and organizing the move carefully are all vital steps in making the transition as smooth as possible.

3. **Strategies for Smooth Transitions:** Building trust and respect among family members, establishing new family traditions, and creating a family mission statement are powerful strategies that help foster unity and create a sense of belonging in the new family structure. These steps provide a solid foundation for the blended family to grow and thrive together.

4. **Mastering Co-Parenting:** Successful co-parenting is about cooperation, effective communication, and developing a plan that prioritizes the children's well-being. Handling conflicts and disagreements with a focus on what is best for the children ensures that the co-parenting relationship remains strong and supportive.

5. **Building Strong Relationships:** Strengthening relationships within

the blended family involves engaging in bonding activities, encouraging open and honest communication, and supporting each child's individual needs. These efforts help create a loving and supportive environment where all family members feel valued and connected.

6. **Addressing Common Challenges:** Blended families often face challenges such as managing jealousy and competition, dealing with ex-partners and external influences, and overcoming financial and logistical issues. By addressing these challenges head-on with clear strategies and a problem-solving mindset, families can overcome obstacles and emerge stronger.

7. **Celebrating Diversity and Unity:** Embracing the diverse backgrounds and cultures within a blended family enriches the family's collective experience. Encouraging mutual respect and understanding, and celebrating family milestones and achievements, helps build a unified family identity that honors each member's heritage and contributions.

8. **The Power of Unity:** Throughout this journey, the recurring theme has been the power of unity. A blended family's strength lies in its ability to come together, despite differences, to create a supportive and loving environment where every member feels a sense of belonging and purpose.

Encouragement for the Journey Ahead

As you continue on the journey of blending your family, remember that challenges are a natural part of the process. There will be moments of difficulty, but there will also be moments of profound joy and connection. The key is to approach each day with patience, understanding, and a commitment to the well-being of your family.

Celebrate the small victories along the way—the moments when a child feels comfortable enough to share their thoughts, the first time everyone comes together for a family tradition, or the day when a new family identity begins to take shape. These milestones are a testament to the hard work and love that you are investing in your family.

It's important to acknowledge that blending a family is a marathon, not a sprint. Relationships take time to develop, and trust must be earned through consistent actions and open communication. Don't be discouraged if progress seems slow or if setbacks occur. These are all part of the journey, and with perseverance, your blended family will continue to grow stronger.

Remember, you are not alone on this journey. Many families have successfully navigated the challenges of blending, and their stories offer hope and inspiration. Keep in mind the strategies and techniques discussed in this book, and don't hesitate to revisit them as needed. Your dedication to creating a loving and unified family will pay off in the long run.

Additional Resources for Support and Information

While this book provides a comprehensive guide to blending families, you may find that additional support and information are helpful as you continue on your journey. Below are some resources that can offer further guidance, advice, and encouragement:

1. Books:
   a. "The Blended Family Handbook: Meeting the Challenges of Blending Families" by David F. Lancy: This book provides practical advice and real-life examples of how to navigate the complexities of blended family life.
   b. "Blended: Writers on the Stepfamily Experience" by Samantha Waltz: A collection of essays from various authors, offering diverse perspectives on the joys and challenges of stepfamily life.
2. Online Resources:
   a. The Stepfamily Foundation[1]: An organization dedicated to supporting stepfamilies with resources, workshops, and counseling services.
   b. Blended Family Success[2]: A website offering articles, tips, and tools for creating a successful blended family.

---

1. https://www.stepfamily.org

2. https://www.blendedfamilysuccess.com

3. **Support Groups:**
   a. **Local Stepfamily Support Groups:** Many communities offer support groups where blended families can connect with others who are going through similar experiences. These groups provide a safe space to share challenges, seek advice, and build a network of support.
   b. **Online Forums:** Online communities, such as those found on platforms like Reddit or specialized websites, can offer valuable advice and support from people who understand the unique dynamics of blended families.
4. **Counseling Services:**
   a. **Family Therapists:** If your family is facing significant challenges, seeking the help of a family therapist who specializes in blended families can be beneficial. Therapy provides a structured environment to address conflicts, improve communication, and strengthen family bonds.
   b. **Co-Parenting Counseling:** Co-parenting counselors can help parents navigate the complexities of raising children in separate households, ensuring that both parents work together effectively for the benefit of the children.

As you continue on your journey, remember that building a strong, loving blended family is one of the most rewarding endeavors you can undertake. With the right tools, support, and a commitment to unity, your family will thrive. Celebrate your diversity, cherish your unity, and take pride in the unique family you are creating.

Glossary

Active Listening

A communication technique that involves fully concentrating, understanding, and responding to what is being said. It helps foster mutual respect and understanding, especially in resolving conflicts within blended families.

Blended Family

A family that forms when one or both partners bring children from previous relationships into a new union. This family structure includes stepparents, stepsiblings, and sometimes half-siblings.

Boundaries

Clear guidelines or limits set within a family to ensure that each member's personal space, responsibilities, and relationships are respected. Boundaries are crucial for maintaining harmony in a blended family.

Co-Parenting

The process by which two or more adults share the responsibilities of raising children after separation or divorce. Effective co-parenting requires cooperation, communication, and a unified approach to parenting.

Cultural Traditions

Practices, beliefs, and customs that are passed down through generations within a specific culture. In blended families, embracing and integrating different cultural traditions can enrich the family's collective experience.

Discipline Consistency

The practice of applying the same rules and consequences across all members of the family to ensure fairness and stability. Consistency in discipline helps children understand expectations and reduces confusion.

Empathy

The ability to understand and share the feelings of another person. Encouraging empathy in a blended family helps build stronger relationships and reduces feelings of jealousy and competition.

Emotion Coaching

A parenting technique that involves helping children understand and manage their emotions by validating their feelings and guiding them through emotional experiences. Emotion coaching fosters emotional intelligence and helps children navigate the complexities of blended family life.

Family Meeting

A regular gathering where all family members can discuss issues, share their thoughts, and plan activities together. Family meetings promote open communication and ensure that everyone's voice is heard.

Family Mission Statement

A written declaration of the family's core values, goals, and purpose. It serves as a guiding principle that helps blended families stay aligned and focused on their shared vision.

Financial Planning

The process of managing the family's financial resources, including budgeting, saving, and preparing for unexpected expenses. Financial planning is especially important in blended families to ensure that all members' needs are met.

Journaling

The practice of writing down thoughts and feelings as a way to process emotions and gain clarity. Encouraging children in blended families to journal can help them articulate and understand their feelings about the changes in their family structure.

Multicultural Celebration

A family event that honors and incorporates the diverse cultural backgrounds of its members. Multicultural celebrations in blended families foster unity and mutual respect while celebrating the richness of different traditions.

Mutual Respect

The practice of valuing and honoring each family member's individuality, beliefs, and feelings. Mutual respect is essential for building trust and maintaining harmony in a blended family.

One-on-One Time

Dedicated time spent with each child individually to strengthen the parent-child or stepparent-child bond. One-on-one time helps each child feel valued and reduces feelings of jealousy or competition.

Open Communication

A key principle in building strong relationships, open communication involves expressing thoughts and feelings honestly and respectfully. It is essential for resolving conflicts and fostering understanding in a blended family.

Parenting Plan

A detailed agreement between co-parents outlining how they will raise their children after separation or divorce. The plan typically includes schedules, decision-making responsibilities, and guidelines for communication.

Positive Reinforcement

A technique used to encourage desirable behavior by offering praise or rewards. In blended families, positive reinforcement helps to foster cooperation and reduce rivalry among siblings.

Role Clarification

The process of defining each family member's role within the blended family structure, including the roles of stepparents, biological parents, and stepsiblings. Clear role definitions help prevent confusion and conflict.

Sibling Rivalry

Competition and jealousy that can arise between siblings, particularly in a blended family where new relationships are being formed. Managing sibling rivalry involves ensuring fairness, promoting empathy, and encouraging teamwork.

Stepparent

An adult who marries or partners with a child's biological parent, becoming a part of the child's family. Stepparents play an important role in the blended family dynamic and must work to build trust and relationships with their stepchildren.

Trust Building

The ongoing process of establishing and maintaining trust between family members. In blended families, trust is built through consistent actions, open communication, and mutual respect.

Unified Family Identity

The sense of belonging and shared purpose that a blended family cultivates over time. A unified family identity is built through shared experiences, traditions, and a commitment to mutual respect and understanding.

This glossary provides key terms and concepts that are important for understanding the dynamics of blended families and successfully navigating the challenges that may arise.